Writhe.Waltz

Writhe.Waltz

Poems by

John A. McDermott

ISBN: 978-1-952326-02-8

Kelsay Books
502 South 1040 East, A-119
American Fork, Utah, 84003

This one, as always, is for Audrey and Christine

Acknowledgments

Thank you to the editors of these journals, where these poems appeared previously.

Forklift, Ohio: "Acid is an Anagram"
Cold Mountain Review: "After Her Affair, We Take a Stab at Reconciliation"
Gingerbread House Literary Magazine: "Captain Hook and Mr. Darling Sitting Poolside"
Steel Toe Review: "Dawn, DFW International"
Treehouse Magazine: "Inappropriate Gifts for Infants"
The American Journal of Poetry: "The Jarred Heart"
Tar River Poetry: "Monopoly"
One Sentence Poems: "Polysyndeton: A Love Story"
Lunch Review: "Report of the Death of an American Citizen"
Seneca Review: "The Russian Doll's Lament"
Juked: "Spring Grove State Mental Institute, Baltimore, Maryland, 1965"
Right Hand Pointing: "There was a Sportscar" and "The Widower as Tourist."
Sport Literate: "Things You Can Roll Through Ray Nitschke's Super Bowl Ring"
museum of americana: "To the Tripping Man at Altamont"
Pif: "Where There are Vipers"

Thanks, too, to Christian Anton Gerard and Justin Hamm for their generosity of time and spirit.

Without the love and support of my siblings, their spouses, and children, none of this would matter. Thank you to them. And most gratefully and lovingly, thank you to my mother, Cornelia McDermott, and to the memory of my father, James H. McDermott.

Contents

Part V *The Jarred Heart*

Part I

Some Boy in a Pack

Dating the Rat King

They are tied together, these boys,
               wrapped up so tight like brothers
      from other mothers, knotted
by blood oaths and anger, a unity
               of a dozen legs yanking in every
      direction, their promises sealed
with spit and filth, the tar of one
               thousand nights and countless curses,
      tail-tied and moving en masse,
and dating one leaves her dating
               them all, prying them apart only
      to see them rewrap and unite.

Yet one boy leaves her with some
        thing better than the plague, he gives
            her this girl-baby and her soul
            spins out like a wheel on fire,
      a million suns of love in a circuit,
and she'd wrestle a pit of snakes
        and writhewaltz with a hive of rodents
            for her daughter to have one simple
               happy life with one good man, unattached
        to any roiling vermin-spokes, no ear
      poisoned by the hissing kiss
of some boy in a pack.

A Stout Boy Waits for His Treat at a Concession Stand in the Toledo Zoo

Our picnic table is littered
with crumpled wax paper and empty plastic cups,
white bread sandwich crumbs and withered watermelon rinds.
My daughter, ten-months-old, sits on her mother's lap
and nibbles a cracker clutched in her fat fingers.

A toddler boy, perhaps two, stands on tiptoes
while his young mother, equally fair skinned, red-haired, freckled,
waits to ask the teen-age counter girl for a snow cone.
His legs are muscular, with shelf-like calves,
and a squat little back like a miniature portrait
of a shot-putter, a Viking, one of those men I've seen on TV
pulling a wagonload of steel kegs up a hill
for a title like *World's Strongest Man.*
They heave things, distances, which other men,

myself included,
could only achieve in another life, with another body,
certainly not this one. This is a boy built for football,
for rampage, and slaughter. I didn't know a tike could be fearsome.
And my daughter glances his way and *coos.*

What say will I have in this?
Now it's more peas, fewer cookies, time for a nap.
Later, it won't be: fall in love with a teacher;
a doctor of medicine; an accountant, an honest one,
not a boy—true, so cute
now—who one day will handily lift kegs, perhaps hurl them,
or stomp on things, ground them with his tremendous thighs.
But why assume the worst? He's a little boy built for tackles,
for keep-away. He hasn't done anything yet.
And I can't keep my girl
from grinning and licking her lips.

Red like Cherry's Radio

Springsteen sings about the boy who hocked it,
       but I want to know what it looked like. I imagine
it's red, like her name, and plastic, but that would be all wrong—
       it's probably silver and black, metal with a faux leather
handle. Cherry bought it in the city, at Crazy Eddie's.
       She brought it back to Jersey on her lap, on the bus, proud
as hell because it cost her fifty dollars, *fifty dollars*—two twenties
       and a ten she didn't have to spend but it sounded so big, not
tinny at all, and she saw herself, right there in the store, standing
       in front of a row of radios, she saw herself with this one
on her bureau, lying in her bed listening to love songs & falling
       asleep with the tunes turned low, like a boy whispering
to her with his head on the pillow right there, close enough to smell
       his breath, close enough to kiss.

And then she met him and at first it was good, good like a song
       she wanted to hum, the melody stuck in her head
whether she wanted it or not, and then it was not so good,
       and then it was pretty fucked up.
I mean, he stole my radio, she told her girlfriends, he stole my
       radio and pawned it, the little turd. Boys with big dreams,
boys with no brains. She is so sick of them.
       And there is nothing he can do to win her back.

And me? I wouldn't steal my wife's radio. Well, there's no radio
       worth hocking. A cell phone? Laptop? What would I trade
for a little cash? There's nothing of hers I could lift for dough.
       But a little dough isn't what I need though that doesn't
make me an innocent, it doesn't mean I shouldn't
       walk right into the bedroom and lay something valuable
before her, like a devoted cat with a dead mouse, like a king with a
       brand new kingdom. All men need something to give their
women. We're all in debt. Which of us doesn't commit some crime

every day? All those little infidelities. The girl at the bus
stop with the rich black hair you want to touch.
   The girl at the bank with the short short skirt

and the long bare thighs. The girl with the smile & the dancer's
   neck you want to lay your head against.
The girl you never see from the front but imagine
   what all as she walks away.
Women know this every time they come to us,
   every time they convince themselves to listen to our songs.
But what is worse: a radio you can get back if you
   just get the cash, or a heart in hock, your predictable lust
for every girl on the street, for every pretty thing that passes.

A Poem about Jayne

The black and white publicity still has her name
printed clearly on the bottom border: *Jayne Mansfield,*
20th Century-Fox player. She's a peroxide blonde lying
on her stomach, her bare legs up in the air, crossed

at the ankles, her chin cupped in her hands, a symmetrical
white smile laughing with us, we here in some place
other than the photographer's studio. I've never lusted
for her, she's not my type, but when my wife tells me

she was decapitated in an automobile accident
I suddenly want to kiss this girl in the photo
though she's far too young for me, this smiling nymph
celebrated and dead before I was born, who wasn't considering

her mortality in this eternal moment, beckoning some invisible
audience in her hair spray and short-shorts, her flesh chilled
by the stage floor, her warm palms supporting her conscious
brain, synapses still firing and connecting, her head still

attached to her healthy body, where it should have stayed.
All life is a movement toward death, I understand that,
this separation of the *then* from the *now* to the *nothing,*
but these abrupt divisions, of blood from body, head

from neck, limb from torso, spirit from flesh, clash
so loudly, in such an off-key din, with our seemingly
permanent presence, we here, her there on the screen,
digitized for us now, our little house in Texas nowhere

near her starlet's California, it's impossible to imagine
her pretty head anywhere but on top of her slender white
neck, nothing sailing through time or space or glass,
never severed ever, for her or me or my wife, for anyone

we love, even as we separate each moment from the next,
from the next, from the next, into this progression that ends
for us all, movie star and minion, the rarified and the common,
the mundane and the spectacular, in the same slashing way.

Benign

When Ed Gein was arrested he had five noses,
dried like flowers, resting in a cup by his kitchen sink.
I think of that as I'm doing the dishes, glancing out the window
over our Texas backyard, green pecans thick on summer branches,
trumpet creepers blaze orange, draped over the wood fence
between our property and our slightly suspicious neighbors.

On my less judgmental days they are fine people.
They have children—just a little unkempt, just a little unruly,
—but they are trying to make their way in the world
just like all of us, one minute after the next, and who am I
to weigh their flaws and fear what may be only in my head?

And then something unimaginable happens in some other
part of the country, in Colorado or Indiana or Arizona,
and then the neighbors trot out their standard lines: *he was such*
a quiet guy and *he didn't seem the sort to kill so many.*
My father was a lawyer in Wisconsin and knew the man who
represented Gein. He had one thing to say about his client:

If you were weary, stepping onto the city bus after a long
day of work and there was an empty seat by an old man
and it was the only place to sit, you'd rest there and you'd chat
with the stranger and you'd get off the bus feeling better,
even lighter, and you'd get home to your warm, well-lit
house, with its dinner smells and laughter, and you'd tell
your wife you met the kindest gentleman today.

The women whose corpses were strung up like deer
in his barn, the women who were born with those noses,
who brushed them with powder, and itched them, and nuzzled
with them, who used them to inhale the scents of their world
would disagree.

I rinse off our breakfast bowls, the toast crumbs,
the sheen of butter from a knife, and worry about my daughter
at school, my wife walking to work. Yesterday our daughter picked
a handful of unimportant flowers unassuming purple blossoms
I can't even name, and they drink from a juice glass,
still blooming, their color vibrant even so near inevitable death.

She didn't mean to kill them when she gathered them
and I didn't think of their death then,
and even now it seems absurd,
but my daughter is beautiful and I love my wife and somedays
there are no fences in the world tall enough
to make good neighbors, to keep us from the ones we suspect
and close our doors upon, to keep us from all the quiet, kindly
gentlemen who seem so benign.

Recognizing the Devil: A Lament

Privy to privilege, sense to senseless,
a mature matinee idol, he doesn't realize
the loss of roses taught, or ought not,
to knock. Knock-kneed girls go 'round
the terrace while terrible terrible ogres
order *bow and kneel once more*—to the cow!
To passing throngs! To granny who can,
but won't, will herself to such subjugation,

will or will not, will o' the wisp whenever
the weathers progress to tempest.
It's maybe-autumn; it's crisp, some cream
or dream charm of semi-automation:
a donut, a do not, a don't, or not yet,
a nutter, a do-nothing, or better-not-get.

On hillside, on streamside, on highway
and shore, all seeds gone seedling
grown so fast, a shoot, a foot, an add-a-pearl
necklace, yet another birthday ammunition,
an admission to toot and own your own horn,
own grand horns or owls galore. Gadzooks!
She's a fruit! of the month! The moth
it tries—must die—it's tough to stay:
so small. So beguile and again begin anew.
A Nick or Not-a-Nick, it's difficult to tell.

The Famous Actor Playing Tevye Curses at the Understudy

for Del

The understudy had once been in the army,
but hazing had seemed simpler then: push-ups
and liquor and the threat of women's clothes.
This he hadn't expected, it was Broadway after
all. Just a boy from Abilene, he hadn't even
known he could sing until the army heard him
and he auditioned for a choir. That got him out of KP
and hauling any weapons. He knew even before
the music he wasn't ever going back south, no,
not that, no. The army was his out. So he went east
and had some luck and now this: he's a villager
from Anatevka though he really grew up with too much
Jesus and too many horses and couldn't care less
about either one so why not call Russia home for a run—
a run that completes his Equity standing and pays more
than any gig ever has. He'll have real pocket money
in his dungarees.

The ritual he hadn't known plays like this:
the dream sequence, choreographed chaos already,
and Tevye turns to the understudy, anyone new,
he does it to them all, and his face contorts, his eyes
burn with the cinder of real pogroms, his charming
baritone bubbles into acid, and he snarls a private
"Fuck you!" at the hapless novice. The understudy's exit
is a stumble off the stage in a daze, walking the right path,
but shame courses through his legs and his head feels light,
light, lighter than it did after anything in boot camp.

He hustles to the assistant stage manager, the narrowly
lit clipboard a beacon, and the man plays along for now,
shakes his headphoned head, and sends him to the stage
manager, a man almost as gruff as the leading player. There
in the hallway, still whispering, he explains how he
must have gotten in Mr. M.'s way, ruined his blocking,
offended him *somehow,* stepped in his light, but he's
at a complete loss, he's certain he's lost this gig,
he sees a blacklist growing, he'll never have another
show on the east coast, let alone the Great White Way,
and he'll be back in Texas before the week is over,

he might as well re-enlist, but this time there won't be
any soft tours with the musicians, there'll be Asia,
someplace with men who hate you and have guns.
At least the star wasn't armed, for all the violence
he felt on the stage, in front of a full house, though
no one in the audience could see the confrontation,
certainly the star would have shot him, gutted him
if a blade had been handy, maybe now
he's planning worse when the scene ends.

The stage manager pats the understudy
on the arm and says, "Forget it, kid. That's
just his way of welcoming you. He does it
to everybody." The understudy wants to cry,
his shoulders release, he breathes again, but
then he remembers his costume change, his
cues coming up. He turns to hustle off to the men's
dressing room and there's another tap.
The stage manager again. "But don't ever, ever

get in his way or he'll have you pitched in one
of the rivers faster than you can say East or Hudson."
And then the understudy truly feels he hasn't left
Texas or the army at all, the *howdy* as a threat,
the Southern hospitality or we'll kill you, the *do it,*
maggot, or you will certainly be sorry, we own you.
It's all right there, the realist thing on the stage,
alive among all these kindly and humble village folk.

The Seduction

What did the Clampetts call them? Cement ponds?
For all our laughing at them, Jed was right.
What else is it, other than a concrete
hole filled with water. I know the moral
arguments against them, why they are wrong,
yet when I see one I want to jump in,
even the indoor, hot-house motel ones,
Holiday Inns in Arkansas, screeching
kids like howler monkeys, slick in discount
bathing suits. But, of course, those aren't my dream
pool: outside, achingly blue, a cool breeze
rippling the clean surface, white lounge chairs,
ample soft towels and a tall iced tea.
It doesn't have to be St. Tropez.

This is merely a backyard in Texas,
yet I know the calculations, the cost,
the carbon footprint of this dinosaur
stomp, the chemical scars, the luxury
when this money could be spent more wisely
on deserving people, more like the Clampetts
before the bubbling crude. All the oil
burned to spark the motor, all the water
shiny and useless, sparkling in the sun.
I want it like a lonely man wants sex,
with a guilt and greed that unhinges bones,
rattles my ribcage and heart, turns my head
to every listing on the realtor's
website, little squares of blue, like acid
to a junkie. You know it's wrong, you do,
but you're already there, in every frame,
hair damp, beads on your cool skin, water-cursed.

Things You Could Roll Through Ray Nitschke's Super Bowl Ring

They always say *golf balls,*
as if this were the universal indicator
that the man's hands were monstrous,
even other-worldly. Take your thumb
and index finger and make the Okay
sign: you get the idea. Holy Jeez,
that's a thick digit. That's a freaking
bratwurst. That's, well, that's one
big old grip, used frequently to grab
other men's jerseys, or thighs, to wrestle
them to the ground, to maybe slip past
a face mask, to jab into the jello
of an eye or twist an ankle deep under
a pile of three-hundred-pound men,
a pile of pulsing meat and sweat and
unguents and gauze and rage.
                            But why
stop at golf balls? There are better things
to squeeze through that circumference,
no? Things more worthy to roll
through that portal, as if Ray's gold ring
could send us to another dimension—
either all-pain or all-pleasure, no domain
of vestal virgins, but, perhaps, as reward
a lifetime supply of venison sausage
and all the Old Milwaukee we could drink.
For punishment, the male reek of the Green
Bay locker room after a Sunday defeat, V.
Lombardi's scathing diatribe still dripping
off moist tile like blood from a crime scene
and the stench—one of mingled shame
and tremendous appetite.

Oh, the things I would push through
this portal: the shrunken head of my most
terrible enemy; a wad of receipts from things
I didn't need (not sending the poor clerks
to Hell, but either myself or some CEO paid
357 times what his lowest employee makes,
yes, let's send him to the Losers' Locker Room
of Eternity). I'd tiddly-wink coins once flipped
Heads when I needed Tails. A matchbook
cover from a wonderful date, one in a series
of wonderful dates, yet each culminating
in disaster. I'd pick up the ring and use it,
a monocle of triumph, a window to gaze
upon success. But when I look: the air
behind the ring is black, a blind drawn
over the porthole, a night sky so moonless
it holds no hope or passage to another
place. It's just an empty space once filled
with tendon and bone and blood.

The Wrestler Makes Weight

by eating a pound of Fig Newtons, the bus soured
by the sleeping reek of twenty boys, some the size of men,
driving through dawn to Chippewa Falls, another Saturday meet.
The smallest one, corded with muscle beneath his letter jacket,
eats in the pink dark of a crowded seat, aging plastic hide cracked
beneath his blue jeaned legs. He unwraps the package, chews,
ignores the taste of damp fruit, the crumbly dough, baked weeks
ago in some factory in Ohio or Pennsylvania, some place down
a different highway than the one he's on, another road and another.
A night years later, he remembers that slow gag through two
sleeves of cookies, through a haze of hours watching television, his
spot on the stained recliner worn, hands wrapped around a wet can
of soda, his belly softer, his hair thinner, but teen-age boy anger
still burning, the need to make someone surrender, to hear
somebody say, "uncle." He gorges again to make weight, to find
some fighting form in mass. This battle will last forever, the news
says, the news says, this national struggle, and he swallows it all,
stuffs it down, devours the words from the screen, telling him to
ready himself, like the broad-bellied coach who baited him, "It's
just a pound, a pound now, don't be a pussy. You can puke later,"
and now it's more than a pound, a pound of flesh added to his
ample gut, in hamburgers and bags of chips, in bile toward
everybody who isn't him, who doesn't think like him. He'll build a
wall of flesh to throw against any stranger unlucky enough to come
against him. He grows there in the dark, massaging those urges,
tending them, steeped in greasy sweat, ready to fight whichever
dusky man they bring to him, whatever woman they tell him to pin,
he'll be willing, his bulk twitching to batter, batter well, bruise and
get bruised, quiver and charge, urged by every bitter appetite.

To a Seagull

The stadium's retractable roof moves on rails
clogged by bolts taken from coastline
construction sites. Pilfering shore birds
drop the odd hardware unintentionally,
but destructively, into the expensive,
carefully wrought gears. Each day
before the roof is closed, a man must walk
the rails high above the green playing field,
the pitcher's mound and the stark chalk lines,
tottering above home, and look for shining
interruptions. The seagulls are not malicious:
they are distractible and careless—
so much like you, my friend, winging through
the clouds, dropping little pretty metal
to fuck up the lives of the unsuspecting below.

John R. Tunis Puking Over a Railing

Boston, 1921

You play tennis against Lengien on the Riviera that summer
and when you return to Massachusetts, drop by the *Globe*'s office
to visit an old Harvard chum, now the Sunday editor, well, when
Winship hears about it, he says the worst best thing: you must
write it, write it now, no choice, today's the day, the paper goes
to bed soon. He needs it before you leave the building.

You are not a writer, but you recognize the opportunity, and say,
okay, sure, yes. *Okay, sure, yes,* and an hour later you're still on
the fire escape no words coming, nothing coherent on the page,
nothing there, and a thousand thousand readers wait, to hear about
the French champion and you, only you, can give it to them, the
details, the afternoon, the ball back and forth across the net. You
lose, of course, she is the great Suzanne, after all, her bare arms
strong, her feet fleet across the clay, you stuck as if in tar.

What does come out as you stoop on the hot black metal is pale
vomit and you wipe your mouth on copy paper and consider your
options. You weigh walking out, telling Winship you can't do it,
nope, not today, hustling out to the streets along the Charles and
letting go of the memory of the afternoon, the condemnation of a
silent Corona, the afternoon of the faraway blue French water and
the thwack of her racket, your back bent and damp with sweat. You
could stare at this American river instead and stifle what Winship
wants. You aren't, after all, Tunis yet, the Tunis to come,
you're just another young man whose father is long dead, the man
who gave you his last name, spurned by his family when he
married your waitress mother, those other Tunis who ignored his
death, not one of them at his funeral.

You're that Tunis, but then, instead, you turn and go back to the
desk, go back to the desk, and it comes, the way it will for the next
fifty years: Tunis on tennis, Tunis on baseball, Tunis on what
makes a ball spinning in the air important, not just to gods,
not just to champions, but to us all.

Part II

The Seduction

No Galatea Has the Upper Hand

Yes, I sort of lied about how I looked.
The photo, well, I took it from a book
about old movie stars. I'm not sure which
one that is. But given the right stitches
I'm certain a good doctor could pull it
off. Maybe Clark Gable? I want to fit
any mold you hold dear. Who would you choose?
Brando, Newman, Dean. I really can't lose
if you go classic. You know how many
stars have fake names? I don't mean like Henny
Youngman (Henny's simply Henry). Cary
Grant changed it all. Each syllable, nary
one from his parents. So, a pseudonym:
something elegant to fit the new him.
The old name he killed with grace and strong bleach?
It was Archibald Alexander Leach.

A man once told him, "Everybody wants
to be Cary Grant." The star didn't taunt
him and say, "Of course." He said, "So do I."
Wasn't he? Or did Archie live a lie?
His early life was filled with tragedy.
When he was nine, his mother went crazy;
they told him she went on a vacation,
but they sent her to an institution.
Then he lied to run off with the circus—
he was just a kid. While the rest of us
at fourteen were in school, he was tumbling,
learning tricks. High wires, ropes, balance beams, things
the rest of us steer clear of, Archie loved.
For lonely men, danger can be enough.

Here's my proposal, if you'll take me changed:
I'll be whomever. I'll have it arranged—
operations, grafts, contacts in my eyes,
diets and wardrobe, sharp razors and dyes.
They'll be my answer if love alone can't.
Everybody wants to be Cary Grant.

There was the Sportscar

There was the sportscar and there was the childseat
and they were at odds. The girl was a surprise.
But the man made it work. And she loved the speed,
left her smelly, limp bear in the seat
while she toddled to daycare and he zoomed to work,
what little zooming he could zoom, and then she was gone
and there was only the empty childseat and the sportscar
and what he wouldn't give to have her back.

What the Parents Don't Want to See

Sonnet for Flight 1183

The little girl was crying in First Class.
She clutched a teddy bear, a doll, a book,
her arms overwhelmed, her red eyes like glass
wet after a sudden rain. So I looked
to see what made her weep—she was alone,
the woman in the uniform her guide.
I imagined divorced parents, the phone
calls between Georgia and Texas. They'd hide
their guilt at shuttling her back and forth
for long weekends, for holidays. This way
they'd keep a safe distance—but was it worth
this scene: her little hands gripping that frayed
bear, that blonde doll, her desperate trust in these
things, the tiny hushed way her voice said *please.*

Risk

This back and forth reminds of a game
I used to play, one I never enjoyed,
one my brother and my college buddies
foisted on me like cheap Italian food,
like the old restaurant you never loved
but everyone else did and you felt bad
for shuddering at the plastic menus

stained and slick with a million fingerprints.
So I'd play, but we'd have to have hours—
it was a choice we couldn't make lightly:
the plastic caskets of colored pieces,
lidded boxes of red and blue armies.
Fights always took more than we expected;
we always lost more men than it was worth.

Now we make grand messes of mundane things,
now every slip of words or choice of friends
is a bigger danger than we foresaw.
Do we really want to commit this time
if I'm not your Western United States,
do I really want to die to make you
my Kamchatka or my Madagascar?

Let's put the pieces back in the closet
stacked box on box near mittens and worn coats,
tiny portraits of the Parker Brothers
on every spine, a pair of patron saints
for all of our battles. Put them away.
These games wear us out and they take too long
and I'm sick of war as recreation.

Play Money

The denominations are always wrong—
gamemakers can't keep up with inflation,
currency fluctuations. One hundreds,
twenties, fives, it's never the actual
cost to pay your electricity, go
to the doctor, buy a whole railroad.
You can buy a real sweet house on Park Place
but it's going to set you back more than you
or the banker (who is not going to be
your good-with-math brother or your keep-it-
fair mother) expected. The banker might
have veiled a fee, but it isn't his fault
the window treatments (treatment's an odd word
there, no?) are pricey and the new neighbors
snoopy. Fresh decorating, cans of paint,
new couches will leave you without one pink
note. The money is a better color
than real American money: pale blue,
yellow, soft purple, dyed like Easter eggs,
springtime pastels. How can this currency
ever fuck up your life? Oh, how it can.
Money this easily spent should come with
death's head designs. What does this play money
have to do with the real thing? It fools us.
Spending it is too easy. Losing it
doesn't hurt enough. You want a hotel
on Virginia Avenue? May I ask
what you know about the business? It's tough
to put people to sleep comfortably.

Especially once they think about all
the bills they've let siphon through their fingers,
flower petals backed by air, so easy
to let them go, and you might think you know
what they are worth or where you can hunt down
more, but you will be wrong on both accounts.

After Her Affair, We Take a Stab at Reconciliation

The taxi clips the soccer ball
and it soars, careens off
the bistro's hanging sign,
bounces, a dull whump-thump,
over the waiter's outstretched hands
and clips the glass carafe. Purple bursts
over his white smock like a gunshot.
This is dusk, our second day in Paris
and screaming, errant objects—suitcases,
kids, dogs, cell phones and cameras—threaten
us everywhere. Cathedrals, alleys, parks.
My wife wonders, "Has everything
gone meteor? Out of orbit?"
"No," I say, "we're just stalked by
causality. There's always a reason. We
just don't know it." We prepare for
our next duck and dodge, and watch
cheap wine seep into stone.

Monopoly

Once upon a time it was all a game,
all for fun, but now the landlords are merciless,
the railroad tracks skewed and overgrown with weeds,
and it just seems a mindless running in circles,
in squares, down the same roads, rich neighborhoods,
poor neighborhoods, they're all ugly and alike,
and the cell seems the destination, a respite, an oasis
for the little dog, the top hat, and the tiny metal shoe.

They have learned to hate each other,
know each other's foibles and ticks too well,
the dog's penchant for pissing by the jail,
the reek of the headband running inside the hat's
broad bell, the click of her heel as the shoe
taps a nervous beat, always on the lookout
for a match. She's soul-sick at being one of a pair.

Utilities are mounting, no cash to pay for light,
or heat, or water, and two hundred dollars
never seems to go as far as it used to, never
like yesterday when rents were manageable
and the dog didn't seem to have the mange,
the silky crown wasn't worn flat and thin,
and her toe wasn't scuffed with ugly lines,
every rock on the road marring her with a scar.

Broken-Headed Goddess

The only thing I've ever won
was in a second grade raffle,

a ceramic statue of Mary,
all in gleaming white,

about eight inches tall.
I carried her home, like a trophy,

on the last day of the school year:
a totem for my crowded dresser

scattered with green plastic
soldiers and Hardy Boy books.

In college she stood in fields
of beer bottles and dank cologne.

One move her neck snapped
and I stuck her head back on

with thick dark glue, a shadow
she wore like a black necklace.

Decades later I smashed her,
like swinging a bat, my last bolt of anger

when we couldn't have a child,
month after month after month

of trying. I threw her bits away,
serene face, clasped hands, folded robes.

And then my wife was pregnant
despite all the doctors' dire speeches.

Mary understood:
she took my wrath and turned it.

Maybe only pagans pray to statues,
or we smash them and they listen.

Inappropriate Gifts for Infants

I wasn't about to bring a yo-yo,
she wasn't going to buy dyes from China,
anything with a sharp edge or poking
or pinching potential, nothing jagged.
We were still childless, but not witless.
We remembered the holiday headlines,
The Five Worst Toys for Toddlers and *The Ten
Recalled Bears That Kill* and *Eight Deadly Dolls*.
But these tiny plastic babies seemed right—
coddled in clear cellophane, cherubic,
both smiling, pink lips and rosy cheeks, peach-
crayon skin, still tinier white diapers—
right for little beds in little houses,
the sort our friend collected, her daughter
would inherit someday, years from this day.

Looking back, yes, they were choking hazards,
temptations to pass little gums and lodge
in her throat, her narrow esophagus.
Maybe this was some sick subliminal
menace we introduced into her house,
her latest addition yet another unintentional
mockery of our empty crib. But, no, we didn't plan
it. They're clearly not toys for play, they're stamped
FOR DECORATIVE USE ONLY in red ink.
But maybe that's just what attracted us,
we understood FOR DECORATIVE USE
ONLY, our girl and boy parts just for show,
nothing to prove they had a true function,
all our intentions coming up empty
month by month by month, year by year by year.
Should she have screamed at us? Nobody died—

one whap on baby's back and the dolls popped
right out of her contorted mouth, like twins.
Even the baby could produce babies,
that's what I saw, when I stooped to the floor,
more newborns, wet and sticky, but all there,
ten fingers and ten toes, and still not ours.

A Sentence Diagram

To long is a verb,
too long is a distance,
combine them in either order—
too long to long,
to long too long
—and there may be a nuance
but the gist is the same,
and I wonder if anyone
quits longing long enough
to notice, except
maybe monks
of the Buddhist
or silently Catholic sort,
or recently and well-fed
sleeping babies, toothless
and smooth jowled,
or the terribly old,
terrible an adjective for aging
not the aged themselves,
too long under the tyranny
of time, caught in a North Korea
of half-remembered song lyrics
and atrophied muscle,
an enforced camaraderie
with the self,
ourselves our too long partner
in this dance marathon.
So monks and babies
and the very, very old—
the rest of us long: long lines
of us long, too long to long,
and yet what else is there
to do but live with a longing
like this.

Life

The top of the plastic white wheel
felt right under my thumb—
I sent its fat numbers spinning
and waited for my route,
every square a random event,
a tax, a raise, a ring.

I always chose the college path,
that was never free will.
School was how my father made it
out of his father's rut.
And though the board rewarded it
it always took longer

to start gathering pink or blue
pegs or to buy a house.
Some games you careened on, empty
and the spins could turn grim.
You had degrees but little else.
Pegless, no spouse or kid,

perhaps it was wiser to wed
young and travel heavy,
too few seats in your little car,
the pegs pushed together
in a crazy, happy huddle,
a full clown car in hand-me-downs,

like the chaos of Christmas break
when you and your siblings
would play these ridiculous games
for days. This was the best,
though boys weren't supposed to be keen
on games without soldiers.

This one felt like fortune telling:
what would the trip look like?
Where would I go? What would I do?
And the wheel wasn't wrong—
I stalled; I had an empty car
for too long and it hurt

far worse than I had ever guessed.
Your car lands on spaces
your fool-self never saw ahead.
A bitter middle-age
longingly looking at babies
in other people's cars.

You drink too much after the news
fertility clinics
tell you and your ever-grieving
wife: chances, slim to none
of ever creating a child
of your own. You're too old.

Too much time on dead-end highways,
though you tried every path,
you picked up every *Doctor's Bill*
and then one December
the wheel decided to give you
the number you'd prayed for.

This is what it tells you to do:
move this many spaces,
pick up the card, and then she's there—
your own big-headed peg,
a pink one and she's beautiful.
Now maybe there's a chance

none of those messier spaces
will haunt you after this.
Maybe the wheel gives you what's right
right now and now there's this:
the three of you can make a life
on this road after all.

Part III

On This Road After All

The Russian Doll's Lament

The smallest Russian doll screams for freedom.
She suffers enclosed spaces badly
and all these layers of painted wood,
hard skin jostling hard skin,
give her the heavy heebie-jeebies.

She knocks, wobbles, and revolts,
alerts the girl she's in, shakes her insides
and that girl says, "Stop it, shrimp."
The next larger one, with vixen eyes and a red kerchief,
sighs. They've done this dance before
and every time she tries to ignore it.

But the long suffering beauty queen
shimmies, too, against her will,
and the next largest girl—woman, really,
if size is the gauge—with portly figure
and matronly gaze, grumbles, mumbles,
lets out a belch: "Settle down," she says,
firm voice directed to her unsettled middle.

The final doll, the front to the world,
the whale to each successive Jonah,
scolds, "I'll deal with you later."
There were still things more pressing to confront
than what was pressing inside her.

I pick them up, pluck them from the dresser top,
the snug set compact, together,
an onion of polished wood and gleaming paint—
woman within woman within woman,
a gift from my wife's mother in Samara.

I hold it out to her, glance at her growing belly,
she as we a pronoun shift which still catches me off-guard,
and she says, in English her own, "You sense the insideness
to come, the companion we made?" I nod.
She smiles at the matryoshka and we wonder
at it all: the culmination, the little mutiny
of birth, the let me out now, the get out please,
to which we all conspire and relent.

The Thirteenth Girl in *Madeline*

Bemelmans made a simple math error,
my wife told me one night: an extra girl.
"There shouldn't be a dozen at dinner.
Who is this girl who snuck past Miss Clavel?
Who doesn't even make it to the sink?
She's vanished by the time they brush their teeth."
"Well, he didn't forget and waste his ink—
Madeline's void was too much. There's relief
in still drawing twelve." "Maybe," my wife said,
"or she broke into the old house. Maybe
she just really wanted to eat that bread."
Watching our daughter, I have a theory:
she's every little girl who's read the book.
She might be you—please, take a closer look.

Horn of Plenty

My daughter unscrews the blue half of the four color pen,
>the plastic front of it in a swollen curve like the hood
of a Bel Air, the white pocket clip on the other side
>a sort of tail fin, the round nub on its end a bumper hitch
or reverse hood ornament. Whoever designed this pen
>was thinking of the Fifties, big cars, Elvis. For a few dollars
anybody's office could have a little luxury.

Four inks: black, blue, red, green.
>I remember the first time I saw one, in sixth grade,
a classmate at our Catholic school had one in his pencil
>case and my single-ink pen seemed diminished, paltry.
Now my four-year-old gazes at its insides,
>the quartet of gold-tipped barrels arranged like a miniature
Gatling gun and she is awed. This mechanism,

not for bullets but for something else, MADE IN FRANCE
>on one side, BIC on the other, this elegant machine
made on a mass scale, is, to her, a wonder.
>And yet mostly I use it for mundanities, circling comma
splices and jotting marginalia in semi-literate college essays,
>when this pen, brilliant before it makes its first mark,
deserves so much more.

Maybe I should reserve it
>for special occasions: grocery lists. Yes, milk and butter
and eggs and fresh fruit. With money in your pocket
>or in your bank account, any trip to a modern American
supermarket is a marvel—strawberries out of season
>and Swiss cheese at any moment and meats, meats without
end. What would the inkwell and quill set say on a tour of Kroger

or Wal-Mart. "So much, so much," I imagine their cries,
       "so much and you don't even see it." It takes new eyes
to see the wonder of your choices.

Don Quixote, Dora, My Little Girl, and Me

The warmth of my daughter's body
on my lap makes sitting through
this dismal cartoon almost worth it.
The animation is chunky, the voices
grating, the singing more shouting
than melodic, the little Latina valiant
and the monkey, shod in scarlet ski
boots, faithful, but so much of the show
drops leaden, its weight delightful
to my daughter but I feel bludgeoned
in twenty minutes. There is one catch—
the map, who, for some reason, seems
voiced by a speedfreak from New Jersey.
I love him, his simple confidence,
his infallible guidance, his keen vision
of the road ahead.
If only life were so straightforward:
follow this way, travel past the barn,
past the trees, ride the boat beyond
the crocodiles, and you will find
your lost treasure. In my journey,
corrupted by fantasy as any mad man
from Spain centuries ago, I've found
fewer rich roads and more dead-ends
than Map has ever mentioned. And he
never says go past the time-clock,
go past the bank, go past the bar,
deny yourself the drink you really
need at five o'clock, or earlier,
or later. He lets us believe there will
always be a clear path to find

what we want, what we need,
and for that, with her warm back
pressed against my chest, her slender
wrist resting on my weary arm,
I am grateful and willing to be fooled.

Captain Hook and Mr. Darling Sitting Poolside

Captain Hook and Mr. Darling, sitting poolside
at the Holiday Inn, smoke discount American
cigarettes and slyly drink cheap gin. Captain Hook
and Mr. Darling are supposed to be watching the water.
It's a Girls' Night Out and their wives have left them
and they feel like two fools and their only comfort
is the buzz of cold liquor and Fleetwood Mac echoing
over the tinny loudspeakers. There's really no such
thing as bad booze or bad Buckingham: it's something on
which they agree. The children's sleek bodies dart in blue
water like pretty pale eels and they each feel a twinge
at recognizing the beauty of wet limbs and motion: this pull
of fatherhood, when neither is known for his affection
or his appreciation of fleeting grace. They even feel slightly
sorry more men aren't here to see these boy-and-girl dolphins,
and each, unaware, separately considers admitting it, aloud—
—oh, wouldn't they be surprised to hear the other speak
 of yet another agreement—but their dark and glistening eyes
catch and they both look away to the lights, to the limp
and dirty sailing pennants draped as decoration, not warnings,
from the high ceiling, the fabric still and straight in the airless
dome, fluorescents humming behind every cry of *Marco! Polo!*
and every Fleetwood beat. Captain Hook holds a plastic
cup—the wrapper was a beast to tear off. He often wonders
what's the point of getting rich when it doesn't buy
his hand back. And Mr. Darling's mustache is dripping
in the heat and he's burned himself twice with carelessly
flicked ash. Yet here they grow pacific. If the women
don't return soon someone's going to say something
they'll regret. No children will die, no, it's worse:

they are too beautiful for death, they've become impossibly
beautiful, oh, good lord, someone's going to cry for pleasure
despite the chlorined-air and terrible tattoos on too many
soft backs. Someone might confess *This, this is not so bad*
and no one really wants to hear that, not Captain Hook,
not Mr. Darling, not even the women out-and-about
or on the lounge chairs watching them from across
the tepid water, watching the man in the topcoat and the other
with the feathers and the brocade, watching and wondering
what devils these men might be, what with their flushed
cheeks, their wet eyes, their soft and subtle smiles.

News from Across Continents

The smallness of the earth
depends upon the people on it,
listening for others' voices,
accented or familiar.

We press our ears on dirt,
against trees, wait for waves
and, keen for a greeting
or a curse—we'll accept either—
build our hearts
big enough to hold
whatever's in the works.

Four Hundred Buried Scholars

I don't know the word
in their ancient language

> for *dirt*
> for *flies*
> for *burning*
> or *sun.*

I don't know the word

> for *nostrils*
> for *bees*
> for *sweat*
> or *sting.*

I can't imagine my limbs
with the weight of earth
upon them

> earth as constriction
> earth as tomb

and I glance around
this room
at the shelves heavy
with books unburned
and wonder:

Would I bear my love
like them

> love of so many words
> I don't even know,
> for which the Emperor

sentenced them
to burial, alive.

Would I bear my love
so bravely?
And what words
would come

like *granules*
like *grave*.

Polysyndeton: A Love Story

for Audrey

And the girl at the breakfast table
has her mother's eyes
and my crooked mouth
and hair like the braid
cut from my grandmother a century
ago, brown with strands of gold,
and once I thought that braid
was disturbing and now
what's disturbing
is this fleeting thing,
and the girl smiles between
bites of cereal
and my heart lurches
like a log truck in a snow storm
too fast on the road for safety,
ice glistening and dangerous
under the wet fat flakes.

The Thirteenth Girl in *Madeline,* Part II

I didn't want the bread. It's no different
than any other loaf in Paris. Even in institutions
we French know *le pain.* It wasn't brushing
my teeth with eleven other girls, that's bound
to be messy, baking soda splatters on our
nighties, elbows shoving at the sinks,
and in the sleeping room, oh, the cacophony
of so many little cows, and all the squeaks
and sighs and gas, the metal framed beds
with mattresses worn flat by the endless
lines of residents before me, no, it wasn't that.
It was no hotel, the vine-covered house,
and *old*, Bemelmans didn't know from old,
until he stepped foot inside the place,
which he did once as far as I know,
to ask about me. He wanted to know
who I was, how did I show up so unexpected.
He knew the other girls, their hair, their
postures, their gaits, though only Madeline
really had his eye. Miss Clavel didn't
remember me, not at first, or so she said.
How could she forget? I was the last one
out of the dining hall and convinced I
was going to make it, to slip in undiscovered,
to eat with them, to sleep with them, walk
to parks and the gardens, to go to the flower
sellers, to learn their lessons, two by two,
and learn their prayers. Bemelmans skips over
the part about it being *school*—there
were lots of lessons: geography and math,
literature and elocution—it was rigorous.

It was not an orphanage. How many
readers ignore that it was Madeline's
Papa who buried her in gifts, the candies
and the dolls. We all had Papas. But she
was spoiled, a brat, to tell the truth, not good
company at all. But I didn't come for education,
the stained bathroom porcelain, or the sour
stink of thin sheets. My own parents
were well-to-do, too, but I was no diva.
I knew my place in the long history
of little girls, my place in line, and knew
a tiger's jaws were nothing to dismiss.

But who would miss me if I were eaten
at the zoo or if my insides burst? The Seine's
current could carry me away and no one
would cry. No one, not my politician
papa, not my fashionable mama, not
my brother, the poet, or sister, the drinker
of coffee and eater of all things chocolate.
Something is not right, that's all I wanted
them to say, and a hawkish spinster
in a habit would do, but she discovered me.
I didn't belong and she wasted no time
in sending me away, my stomach heavy
with their passable repast, my tiny
feet leaden as I headed for my bed,
so much finer, so much plusher than any
in that old house. I wound up in my
warm and gilded room, and certainly,
to anyone else, nothing was amiss.

William Blake Visits La Discotheque

You found in the confusing pages
of your sister's second year French book,
wrapped in brown paper and covered in Magic Marker
rainbows, the spine broken in defeat,
and the onion-skinned poems of her World Lit anthology,

that Wolfman Jack, too, spoke low of forbidden love
while the red light on your transistor burned—

silver hand-held Japanese radio,
multitudinous container of multitudes—

and somewhere far from crowded dance clubs
throbbed throbbed throbbed
your heart,
your cramped bedroom closet like a dank cove
filled with foreign verbs and strange stanzas
aimed toward the Palace of Wisdom.

Nothing to Prove

The Romans offered him
some wine with myrrh to dull the pain,
a kindness, I suppose
from the soldiers sent to kill him,

the drink their century's
notion of an anesthetic.
I can't believe it would
do much to ease the agony

of sharp metal through flesh,
of heat and height and jeering crowds.
I can't even pretend.
Of course, I'm not as strong as Christ—

but the thought of crucifixion
is one I can't conjure
clearly. Consider medieval monks
whipping themselves bloody,

pain a path that made sense
to link their bodies' wounds with his.
And in the Philippines
there are enthusiastic men

ready for a passion
of their own, no Romans needed.
Imitating his pain
seems the goal but for what reward?

Which king brought myrrh to him,
in Bethlehem, how did he know
dull pain would be a gift
fit for a child thirty-three years

away from the waiting
cross? Was it prescience, prophesy,
or just a bit of luck?
Yes, we are all headed for grief,

every breath give us
another chance to find some way
to ache. No wise man brought
myrrh to my birth but I wouldn't

have the strength to deny
the offer of a sedative
before they broke my heart,
or, first, my body and spirit.

Give me liquor or pills,
I would need some shroud, a thick veil
to lay between my nerves
and the bite of every hammer.

He couldn't ease the pain
and still speak to us as human—
it's authenticity
for God to choose to hurt like us.

So why endure our pain?
I'll never be a deity
and see no sense in scars
to prove my human frailty.

Knock me out, let me sleep,
bring on the pacifying tricks.
The last drink I deny
might be the one I really need.

The Genius of Otis

Its genius isn't the elevator's rise
but the more careful descent, the steady
decline to stop the car from free fall.

It's one to thing to go up, to save the steps
it takes to climb a flight or two or ten;
it's another to prevent the crushing

splayed bodies should sagging chains careen,
story after story of empty shaft,
settling with a sudden smash of wire and dust.

To Mr. Otis, late of Chicago:
we thank you every time the door opens,
closes, every time we push a button
and we climb and climb, and safely return.

Part IV

Bent on Love & Demolition

To the Tripping Man at Altamont

December 6, 1969

Werewolf, caveman, California bear
fresh from the northern woods, you
stand beside Mick Jagger. The camera
trains on you, though you don't see it.
You see—what? Whatever acid burns
in your brain turns you inside, away
from the music, oblivious to the biker
in front of you, the man paid in beer
to keep the crowd away, or, as the day
wears on, to keep them, at least, at bay.

How did you end up on the low stage,
not one of Hell's Angels hassling you?
Did you come from behind amplifiers,
did you leap to escape the jostling crowd,
the vibe gone wrong, wrong, Meredith
Hunter not dead yet, but soon, a verse
or two, before this song is through. If this
were John Bunyan's tale, New Pilgrim's
Progress, you would be Anguish, capital A,
tongue worrying & working your mouth,
heavy hands stroking your bearded face,
gripping your long hair. Your shoulders
slump. You lose your denim jacket. Your
shirt's paisley, perhaps, or is it camouflage?
Do you know the way to San Jose or Saigon?

And what do you see that's worse than this,
this crowd ready to tear at the bikers,
the bikers ready to lash out at the crowd,
these gods of rock made lower case g's
with the sweat of their fear, their jangling
notes, their earlier pleas to the crowd, please

let's just all get along (no thought of spending
the night together, let's just get out of here
alive). Most of you do—not Meredith—but
maybe you live to see this footage? Do you
remember? What was your vision? Barren
farmland, stolen water, concrete highways,
napalmed jungles, warm water in oil drums,
Ronald Reagan and his celluloid chimp,

the glass of a million flat-screens glinting
in a 21st century landfill, Youtube, us,
horrors you can't explain, for which words
don't yet exist. Or maybe it's simpler.
Your mother dying in a gray nursing
home, your father's grave, your sisters,
your brothers too far to hold your hand.

Please, somebody hold your hand, this
is no place for a bad trip. Now: the biker
notices you, grabs your shoulder, another
yanks you offstage. They curse you
and you disappear into the roiling bodies.
Mick keeps singing about power, about
power, about power but he's not the one
who has it here, not here: it's diffused,
it's nobody's and it's anybody's, and the boy
with the gun has only minutes to live but
nobody knows that yet, not the camera,
not the band, not the white girl in the crochet
vest, but the blade has already jabbed in you,
it's warm from the stabbing a chorus before.

Patience, Please

ekphrasis for Ethan and Keith

The rock star's aviators reflect
the photographer in rectangles of white
light. It's impossible to tell who else is there,
but we are. He looks our direction, to future us,
us whoever happens to glance his way.
Keith's solemnity belies his jaunty scarf,
his denim shirt, its stitched patches—COKE,
the cartoon tongue, those kissable red lips.
A Drug Free America Comes First,
the sign behind him proclaims. Lo, we
ask with the guitar player's nudging:
before what? Before what?
The photographer wants to tell us.
Keith wants to tell us.
What comes after?
Patience, please.

Nirvana Playing Twister With the Smashing Pumpkins

a Boston bar, 1991, the week of the release of Nevermind

Right hand on blue, Darcy tells Krist.
       He's naked save his blue underwear
              and slippery with Crisco smeared
                      across his chest and belly.

Kurt, in jeans and a long coat, volunteers
       to go second. "Left hand on yellow,"
              she tells him. Dave wants clarification,
                    "So, you mean…" and James Iha stands
                    abashedly behind him.

It sounds like a dream, nostalgic
and surreal, but it's there:

       Jesus, I spend a lot of time on the internet
       watching useless shit. (And, yes, this is a prayer,
       whether Jesus knows it or not, is familiar
       with the internet or not, whether he knows
       when I speak of Nirvana I mean, not, paradise
       but a rock band from America)

       Does He know what I mean by America? I've never
       understood
       how we, and by we, I mean, Americans (see
       how fucked up that is?), use *America* to mean us,
       the U.S. (capital Us, right?) and not Canada
       or Mexico or all those other countries with an equal
       right to be called America. I digress.

And Twister, it's a game, not a tornado, not like the one
that swept up Dorothy or routinely decimates rural
America (there I go again) but the game on the plastic
mat with the colored dots—yellow, red, blue, green—
a road map to awkward yoga and sexual embarrassment.

      "What are you doing?" the woman from MTV asks
            Krist. "The rules are simple," he says. "You need
                a can of Twister and some, ah, Crisco."

What are the surprises here? Billy Corgan with hair.
Darcy looks healthy and Veronica Lake-ish as she spins
the needle and calls out, so politely, the moves.
      I've wanted to write about Kurt for so long,
      But could never get it right, never say the right
      thing, whatever it was that needed to be said,
      added to the million words already said,
      the funeral pyre of eulogies and record reviews.

But here it is, and the metaphor is Twister.
What turns your life upside down? Fame. Junk.
Money. Something unnamed burning inside.
But it's so much simpler to blame the woman
at the board. (Some people call her Courtney
but it's more than that.)

      Where do any of us end up? Ass over teakettle,
      my mother used to say, and who used teakettles
      in 1991, let alone 2019?

              Maybe it is nostalgia,
to watch it, maybe the most pointless three minutes
of Youtube ever, more pointless than cute cats
or adorable children or countless hordes winning

Darwin Awards, but you've watched a lot of bad
footage: housewives on acid, gangs fights, tutorials
on broken dryers. Maybe it's therapy to watch
someone you never knew but seem to mourn now
even more than you did then—

                              —and the plastic sheets,
              two of them (Dave asked if players were supposed
to use both and Darcy said yes) end up on Krist, after
                         everyone tumbled, the sound of the crowd
                  and the wet plastic what you're left with, all these
boys and girls so fucking young and Jesus, us, still twisted,
                              trying to figure it all out.

Where There Are Vipers

Los Angeles, 1999

This was during the bloom of Y2K panic:
the girl in the silk pencil skirt sips chartreuse,
its eerie green glowing in the flickered
light tossed and retossed from the red candle
in the center of the crowded table.
Years before the young actor had seized up
on the sidewalk outside this greasy club
but no one talked of River anymore.
Where there are vipers there is always sleep
and where there is sleep there is forgetting.
The olive at the bottom of her first cocktail
languished without the vermouth and gin,
drained by the unemployed bass player
minutes before. "Bella donna," he'd said,
"isn't for dreams. It's used for solutions."
She imagined solutions suspended
in laboratories across the Valley
where her problems floated like lemon garnish
in so many drinks in so many bars
not so different than the one right here.
A voice from the kitchen cut through the din,
laughing, something about the Rio Grande,
crossing it hard and still surviving drought.

Acid is an Anagram

Lysergic Acid Diethylamide

Third act sad lads telegram:
Adam. Midas. El Cid & Sal M.
The glad ladies: Dyads. Edie S.
They lead me. They rise & add gears.
This is dice day—here is the camera,
here is a diagram. Say yes, yes!
Dial clear rays, said Death. Lame,
red-clad mice. Either case, see dear
Dad, thy dead Dad. Eh, Hamlet?
Silly drama, said Death. So silly. Let
the gel set. Death—my ally? Or theirs?
A cage & a race. A mighty ride.
Get real. Slay ideals. Stay here.
Right here. Dream,
they said. Dream.

Spring Grove State Mental Institute, Baltimore, 1965

On Sixty Minutes with Charles Kuralt

In Cottage 13, the acid experiment begins,
fourteen hours under their eyes.

Peg M., middle-aged mother of two,
Peg M., wife to the husband
      who had her committed.
Peg M., who feels fake,
      has felt fake since the births
      of the boy,
      of the girl.

What Peg M. says in the beginning:
my father called me his little faker,
      his little fakir,
      fake is what I feel.

In Cottage 13, the doctor tells her,
"Look at the rose—"
      "—if I want to," Peg M. says.

If I want to.

What Peg M. says next:
Shut up and listen to the music.

What Peg says next:
I don't know what, but boy am I afraid.

What Peg M. says next:
I could tell you about women.
They think *there goes beauty,*
there goes love and they're scared to death.

87

When you cry you don't just cry for yourself,
you're crying for your daughter,
her daughter, and the ones that come.

What Peg M. says later:
What's transfiguration mean?
      I feel reborn.
      I feel beautiful
      I feel squashed but beautiful
And I found God.

What did you say, girl? (the husband asks)

I said I found God.

I found a great big hunk of creation.

                What did you say, girl?
                What did you say, girl?

A week after this, she was released.
intones the narrator, *released,*
says Charles Kuralt, *from Spring Grove.*

        Charles Kuralt, Charles Kuralt
        What is this business you're in?
        What do you think of Peg M.?
        What do you think of the mister?
        Tell me—
If I want to.
                What did you say, girl?

Later, later,
Peg M. dyes her hair & meets her grandchild
& her daughter looks just like her.

Peg M. is happy.
No, really, she's fine. Fine.

The doctor says,
      This drug is serious business.
      This drug is serious business.
      This drug is serious business.

      Look at the rose,

if I want to, Peg M. says.

Shut up and listen to the music, Peg M. says.

I don't know what, but boy, am I afraid.
I feel reborn.
      I feel beautiful
      I feel squashed but beautiful
And I found God, Peg M. says.

I found a great big hunk of creation.

This is Government Research, Decades Old

The LSD interviews, Los Angeles, 1950

The anonymous housewife from L.A.
trips, while the man in the suit asks questions.
Above the man she looks, above the man:
I wish I could talk in Technicolor.
She has a lovely neck and her eyes gleam.

This is government research, decades old.
The footage is black and white, while she dreams,
the anonymous housewife from L.A.
Does anybody know where she wound up?
Does anybody know where she wound up?

She has a lovely neck and her eyes gleam,
the anonymous housewife from L.A.
Above the man she looks, above the man,
the footage is black and white, while she dreams:
I wish I could talk in Technicolor.

Does anybody know where she wound up?
Above the man she looks, above the man,
the anonymous housewife from L.A.
trips, while the man in the suit asks questions
trips, while the man in the suit asks questions.

The footage is black and white, while she dreams;
this is government research, decades old.
Does anybody know where she wound up?
The anonymous housewife from L.A.
The anonymous housewife from L.A.

I wish I could talk in Technicolor
I wish I could talk in Technicolor
I wish I could talk in Technicolor

Acid & the Observatory

Lying on the brown grass of Griffith Park
you're Mineo shot down without bullets
—save the ones tracing jagged neon paths,
all of your synapses under fire.

You're Mineo shot down without bullets,
what path you take is not yours for choosing,
all of your synapses under fire:
relinquish, release, there's nothing to it.

What path you take is not yours for choosing
—fingernails, first fucks, flaming marshmallow—
relinquish, release, there's nothing to it.
memory is just electric current.

Fingernails, first fucks, flaming marshmallow
—save the ones tracing jagged neon paths.
Memory is just electric current
lying on the brown grass of Griffith Park.

Report of the Death of an American Citizen

It has rained every day for three weeks
and traffic splashes, wet whirrs, beyond
the window as I study this form, again
and again, looking for something like meter
or soul or beauty, again and again, and nothing.

(I'm not going to write about Sylvia.)
(I'm not going to write about Sylvia.)

Let us consider the other Americans who died
abroad, not the woman, whose occupation is listed
as *Writer* on the faded paper stamped on the top
in sans serif font DEPARTMENT OF STATE,
not the woman buried in Heptonstall, Yorkshire.

Remember the office manager, the salesman,
the high school biology teacher, the student
abroad for a semester. Where were they born,
only to die in England? Topeka or Spokane?
A suburb of Baltimore or turquoise Santa Fe?
                    Let us not think about Boston,
or the kitchen of 23 Fitzroy Road, or her less-famous
name, two of the few handwritten words
on the otherwise typed form: *Hughes, Sylvia.*
(Another handwritten word in the top
right corner of the page: *file.*)

What does fame bring her? Strangers reading
this bureaucratic assessment, strangers intruding
on clerical moments beyond her consciousness.

Informed by telegram:Copy of this report sent to:
Traveling or residing abroad with relatives or friends,
as follows:

The information and data concerning an inventory
of the effects, accounts, etc. ~~have~~ *has been placed under*
File 254 in the correspondence of this office.

Here, inside, away from the rain:
      a PDF on the internet,
      a phrase as anti-lyric
      as it would be foreign,
      to the deceased in 1963

tells me the disposition of her effects:
In custody of husband.

What is this drive to find an ode? Casual voyeurism
or morbidity or strange affinity or curiosity or love
of language in odd places (in blackberry brambles,
in the cry of newborns) on forms filed in triplicate
on onionskin then scanned decades, yes, decades,
after death.

It's not like we didn't know she was dead.

And here's more proof: the Vice Consul knows
she's gone. Mr. Carter signed it, on March 1.
Her passport (*No. 1746223*) is cancelled
and why should we care or feel sorrow, for her,
if not for the office manager and the salesman,
the biology teacher and the student,
as well, addresses and passport numbers
unknown but for their lack of eloquence

while breathing. Oh, breathing. It's so much
more than words and it's so much more than this.
It's more than Carbon Monoxide (*domestic gas*),
(it's a gas, gas, gas, the Rolling Stones will sing
only a few years later, in English of a different sort
of bitter), or traffic accidents, appendicitis, which used
to kill so many and now is relatively benign, or lightning.

Why don't we write about them?
We don't even know their names.

I wasn't going to write about Sylvia,
(Mrs. Hughes, to you, stranger)
but none of these answers feel complete
and if I can't find her here on the page
or deep in the dirt of Heptonstall, she still
feels here in a Texas she never considered,
resurrected in today's rain, days and days of it,
cleansing and burdensome and necessary
and exhausting, something she might find
comforting, even worthy of praise, or rather,
still, harrowing and familiar.

Oscar & Kurt in Reading, England

What I know about Reading, I learned
from a man in jail: *g-a-o-l,* he spelled it—

& one hundred years later, it's the same
sky tented above the festival as had lifted

above the gallows built for the wistful
man, condemned for *killing what he loved,*

Oscar tells me. Lord, one more murdered
girl & what couldn't she give him, I wonder,

and why does the poet lament the killer,
& not her, the silent corpse behind it all?

Oscar conflates them, makes them one,
lover-to-lover, as bodies do, but homicide's

not suicide, no matter how he spins
it. Kurt comes out differently, wheelchair

& hospital gown (another man out of a cell)
but armed with a guitar, not a gun (this

time). There's a light show of stars & strobes
& as the trio plays their most famous song

a 4th young man careens across the stage
spasmodic among the musicians, marionette

to their music, while Kurt winces & groans:
a denial, a denial, a denial, a denial.

Years later, the dancer calls it *punk as fuck,*
set free up there, a man wild on request,

the band wanted him there, no stage crasher,
& Oscar tells us, scribbling from his view,

some sell, others buy, & each man kills
the thing he loved, as if he prophesized

us & the crowd & the dancer, all delirious,
& Kurt, keening, bent on love & demolition.

Part V

The Jarred Heart

So Come The Birthdays Of Beloved Dead

So come the birthdays of beloved dead
we celebrate them though they are not here
and do not know where crossing Lethe led.

We hope chilled gin and opera fill their heads,
some lark-like soprano is what they hear,
when come the birthdays of beloved dead.

Yet years pass and we'll want them here instead,
though sorrow in this world is sure as tears
and we know not where crossing Lethe led.

Perhaps our tears of grief are idly shed
when heaven bursts with friends and few are here.
So come the birthdays of beloved dead

the last of the living bear all the lead:
memories gain mass with the passing years,
and we know not where crossing Lethe led.

Weep once for them and twice for our kindred,
who long for their day of death to draw near
when come the birthdays of beloved dead,
though we do not know where crossing Lethe led.

A History of This Hotel Sofa

Chinese-made, a million identical,
it crossed the Pacific padded and boxed,
on the deck of a cramped container ship,
a hundred tons of furniture and toys
headed for Los Angeles and beyond,
then ended up here in Room Nine-Fifteen,
brother and sister and cousin couches
on every floor of this Houston hotel.
I lie in the dark not dreaming
while my wife and daughter—six and spindly—
snore on the big bed down the short hallway.
This is a suite. I'm in the living room,
if that's what we'll call it, and sure, it fits.
Ponder the abstract nouns this couch has seen.
Desperation, lust, anticipation,
fear. Happiness, frustration, and surprise.
Nights before interviews, days of weddings,
ill-considered affairs and hospital
treks. It's a good spot to steep in worry,
a landing place for a fresh sharp flash of fear.
My bare feet hang off the end. I'm too tall.
Who has cried here, made love here, lain awake
here before?
         Long ago, the Egyptians
didn't only mummify the wealthy.
They preserved seventy million corpses,
holy cats and birds of prey, attendants,
their average Joes and their Living Gods.
A barge's journey to the Other Life,
crowded with pharaohs and millers and me,
adrift on these cushions where other souls
have waited or wondered, or worried, too,

about their kids or their jobs, their broken
parts, the broken parts of this couch, metal
frame jabbing beneath rough, mottled fabric,
while we—suddenly those strangers are kin—
consider life from a prone position.
Thousands of couches in as many rooms,
exponential temporary dwellers
desperate, maybe alone, and lying here
waiting for an answer or something else:
maybe just an iced drink or one safe sleep.

Southern Vision

for MJM

Flannery O'Connor raised from the dead,
her balance skewed, her crutches lost.

Listen! *Ghosts can be fierce and instructive,*
she whisper-drawls. I strain for what she's said.

Ghosts can fierce and instructive. I wait.
Yes, I believe. Flame halos, slashing swords.

But, then—she's a woman. A faded housedress.
Behind her, peacocks scream in the fogged light.

She is no Gabriel, no harbinger
of doom, just one of us: American,

blighted by history, forced from the tomb,
stumbling across a crumbling land.

The Widower as Tourist

The adobe goat—russet and prickly—
in frozen dance outside the tchotchke store

in Albuquerque, forever bounding, forever
braying, stabbed the orange-black dusk

with his leap though the sidewalk was still
as a midnight church. Where had all the people

gone? Everyone else was far away, to celestial
spaceships and dimly lit bedrooms, skydiving off

our Earth, and here I was left, like this silent bleating
statue, his flight thwarted in fired mud, pinned to concrete,

envying his attempt at escape but kin to his capture.

Dawn, DFW International

The note above the urinal written on a blue Post-It
told me *NO H20!* I side-stepped down a few tiled feet
like solo Fred Astaire, where a chunk of chewed gum—
pale pink and rigid—sat forlorn next to the drain.
I was alone among the mirrors and empty green stalls,
but not alone. The janitor with the black Sharpie
told me where to go with his scrawl and the man
who'd spat out the once-sweet-now-flavorless wad,
perhaps he sat in seat 17B to Tokyo or Duluth right then
and pats his coat for the rest of the pack. *You want a piece?*
he'd say, and I'd say *no, but thank you* and go back
to my paperback or crossword. The third stall
so covered in rust it looked ancient, the First Urinal
of the First World, ceramic under tribulation, through tribes
of traveler upon traveler, the endless procession of men
voiding coffee and coke and Gatorade, vodka, tap water,
beer, and Perrier. Where are they now, these men
of the world? To homes and cubicles and bedrooms,
and cars. To cars: Toyotas and Chevys and Saturns and Kias.I'm
done. I want to brush my teeth, tongue heavy
with cheeseburger and fries from the chain restaurant
on Concourse B but I don't have the right tool. I travel light.
The mirror clears, freshly wiped, and behind me a hundred
faces stare, some smiling, some weary, one weeps:
too long on the road, too many days away from his wife,
his child. I raise my hand to them, an index-finger
pistol and wave once in hello, and goodbye, and see you
later alligator and until we meet, and never meet, again.

This Is the New Year

Gassing up my mother's car at midnight,
late January snow swirls around me.
The neighborhood convenience store shoots light
across the lot. I wish the gas were free.
I peer through the windows papered with sale
signs, teenage cashiers dying of boredom.
Taped on the pump there's a scrawled note, smudged, pale:
"Great pay and occasional explosions."
This is the New Year. My father is dead.
I'm here, but school started a week ago.
My mom says, "Can't you get it through your head?
He's gone." And I'm stuck back in Ohio,
too late to help, too late to leave, and here's
a job. My plan: forget school, forget tears.

The Little Man on the Mantel

The little man on my mother's mantel
is more than a century old, a statue
from England, a Victorian tchotchke
dramatizing the evils of drink. One side
he's dapper, a real gentleman—a fine
hat, a neat coat, a sturdy cane.
Turn him around and he's a clown,
not the happy sort. His clothes askew,
his red cheeks burning, here is the Jekyll
and Hyde of alcohol. He's labelled
on his painted base: GIN and WATER.
You can guess which is which.

As a kid I thought he was funny, a little
creepy. Now on summer afternoons— after five,
always we wait 'til after five— I find him
soothing. I raise my sweat-beaded glass
and give a silent toast to his sotted self and sip,
a little Tanqueray, maybe Bombay, a little
medication tempered with tonic and lime. I won't
go too far: two most nights, three at tops, never
four or more. Cut me and I'm mostly water,
but a shot of fermented grain, a sprig of juniper
and a host of spices assembled in Great Britain
and imbibed in this united state and I'm at liberty,
never mussed, my gaze bright, my tie still straight.

I'd never go too far because I wouldn't want
to ruin one of the best things about breathing.
Remember weighing the next move to kiss
the girl or not, wondering if it would ruin a good
friendship to lean over at the right moment
and brush your lips against hers? Or further on,
if good sex would later make for bad blood?

Oh, booze, oh, I wouldn't want to lose you.
I watch the men on the mantel and moderate
my every move. Like happy clockwork she can
be yours, a gleam in your eye, a smile on your ready,
parted lips. Cheever gave it all a bad name, found sorrow
when he took it too far. A pity. The trick to loving
gin is staying loose but holding fast and never,
ever spinning the little man to his sadder, sorrier side.

On Reading We Have Always Lived in the Castle While Packing Up My Parents House of Fifty-Three Years

Buried dolls are imperfect talismans; row
after row of preserves are not preservation.
I, too, remember my sisters' toys as sacred,
my family food as both strange and sacrosanct.
Don't eat what strangers offer: it will kill you.
A book nailed to a tree, a book like you,
a book like me, and rhubarb is delicious and two-fold,
pretty and poisonous. Who is Gloucester to King Lear,
friend or foe? Who is constant for Constance?
Merricat. And I am the strange younger child, too.
Three words—melody, Gloucester, Pegasus—
to keep Merricat safe. Song, sinner, horse.
I steal Merricat's words to keep me shielded
but as with her, they never really work.
Not really. But what is real after all? A childhood
bed. A dining table. Portraits on the painted walls.
Or a burning house. A maddening crowd. Ghosts
of the Dead returned. Cardboard boxes of holiday
ornaments, of dusty volumes, of spoons and butter
dishes. Did your father sing that day? I have no head
for song like him, says Uncle Julian, all our uncles grown
groggy and fog-bound, blighted like him, by the past.
We pack up my mother's house, no castle but a home
for five decades, all my life. What can I bury to preserve
this place? Nothing. I am not Merricat. Not brave or rash
enough. There is no arsenic in my sugar bowl, all of this
ceramic wiped clean, clean of anything that chokes or stings,
stops clocks, or even heals, and who would I want to murder
anyway? No one does crime like time, row after row, and who
—not Merricat, not me—doesn't smolder or gag on that?

Here Is Much Water

Here is much water, the Baptist preacher said,
his arms open and raised. *What are you waiting for?*
He'd just dunked the young woman in the waist-high
pool at the front of the church and for a long moment
the congregation was silent, considering. This is Texas.
I am not Baptist, but lapsed Catholic from the North,
raised in the Church of my father, a man who remained
faithful all his eighty-three years: faithful to Rome,
faithful to Dublin, faithful to the law—his profession—
and his wife—his love. He told us he'd learned to hate
the English at his mother's knee, a hate he carried long
but which didn't stop him from marrying an American
girl named Banks, a surname born not from the Shannon
but the Thames. I am the child of an isthmus, raised
between Mendota and Monona, but emigrated—
or banished—to the southland of catfish creeks
and, for the better off, swimming pools. There is much
water but none of it feels mine.
                    Faith is memory, the preacher
said, the tales we share, the Bible and the family,
but I no longer trust humans and the Good Book,
the Good Book used for so much bad, yet I trust stories
and I trust water. The water my father's parents crossed,
leaving Galway Bay, across the wide Atlantic; the lake
my ancestors worked, mighty Superior; and the waters
I've crossed—the Mississippi and the Arkansas, the Brazos,
and the Red, and the nameless snaking bayous. My father
is dead fifteen years and whether he's crossed Lethe or not,
I remember him, his gab and eloquence, his hate and love,
and he taught me enough to pause and look behind me.

Now, look, behind you: Great Michigan, lake of many
people, Potawatomi and Swede, Ojibwa and Italian, roiling
or pacific, here is much water, and it is mine and it is ours,
as much ours as the water we drink, brewed with hops
or mixed with whiskey, steeped and sugared into sweet tea
or kept simple and cold with a cube of ice. Here is much
water, to wash with and to journey over. This is not Erin
and I don't live by you, Michigan, no longer a young man
in Milwaukee, but you are there, as surely as God was there
in every molecule for the girl and the preacher. My god
of water and love, teach us to be wary of what we learn
at anyone's knee unless it is the sympathy and the strength
to keep us, and anyone with their hands up, from drowning.

The Jarred Heart

I.

The heart is the well of our thoughts
        the Ancient Egyptians believed
and so it was returned to the body,
        the torso packed with clean linens
surrounding the wine-cleansed organ.

The kidneys, the intestines, the liver,
        and the stomach: those travelled
to the Other Life safely in canopic jars.
        undecorated in the earliest instances,
then later painted with gods' heads
        and human faces.
Now not Hapi or Imseti, I imagine, but NFL
        logos, brand names: the red Target
and M & M's. Mine would be all eyebrows,
        Muppet-like, gaping front teeth
and hard chin, no representation of deity,
        only me.

But my heart is not yet housed in stone
        or slipped from beneath my ribcage
and washed in wine,
        grapes not crushed by the feet
of Hebrew slaves
        but pressed in stainless steel vats
in California or Chile,
        the blended red sold for ten dollars
a bottle in the Kroger on University Drive.

II.

My daughter, six and fair,
          lies in the kitchen on the red brick floor
with arms and legs still, smiling death,

          the library book *Mummies* cast a foot
from her warm, slender body,
          her running blood still housed
in her soft white flesh.

She confuses mummy with zombie
          and rises from the dead,
cherubic pretend cannibal,
          and this is the Day of Thanksgiving.

A million mummified birds buried
          in a single cemetery
their leathery hides crammed in our living room
          pressed against the tall windows
looking out onto Raguet Street
          feathered carcasses stacked on the mantel
where the candles used to stand
          stacked in row of black gray row
where the couch used to go,
          the couch I sit on with our girl
with the library book in her lap
          reading about one million mummified birds
in a single cemetery.
          And they were here, crowding us, airless room,
and they were gone, the room our own again,
          space between us on the cushions,
between the fabric and our flesh and the piano
          across the bare floor, uncrowded, unlittered

with the pressure of sacred corpses,
        a metroplex of holy birds.

"What does preserved mean?" she asks.

III.

And if you took my lungs
        and washed them in that same wine
what air would rinse away and into what
        sink would the red wine run?

The oxygen of my chest pressed against
        my first lover, my naked boy
flesh warm against hers, warm in the bedroom
        of her October-aired apartment
and I enter her, the first time, our first time.
        That air in my teenage lungs has lingered
like love, like loss, for three times our age then
        and more, not out of remorse but remembrance,
that air, that air again, that air again,
        and what other molecules of other lovers,
of sex and laughter and sickness, of decades
        gulped while heaving
in hotel bathrooms, in Iowa and Indiana
        and Illinois,
the strain of vomiting salmon or Scotch—

but wait, there is a place for the stomach,
        we will get to that jar, that sacred organ
of grinding and regurgitation—

no: this is the place for air,
          first air of first days, and all the deep inhalations
of cigarette smoke in my mother's house
          or my favorite dark winter bars
what streams of scent and exhalations
          snake about our conscious makings.

IV.

"Daddy, I will say what happens to you:
          You will be dead, but you will not burn.
          I will turn you into a mummy and put you
          In a coffin and slide you into a wall,
          Behind a door, here in this house, upstairs,
          And you will always be here.
          And I won't tell Mama."

And though this sounds like a horror movie
          she speaks of love
her blue eyes sparkling,
          and she raises one finger
a *Hark, I hear* gesture,
          and says,
"What did you want to happen?"
          as if I could see no better future
for my body than carved out and leathered
          and stored in some dark crevice
of our home in my exile in Texas
          with a girl I love
who loves me.

(She told me so today, clutching my face
in both soft hands, "I love you I love you

I love you I love you I love you I love you
even
when you don't say I love you back.
But I know you do and will forever."
And I want her never to let go
and I think six-year-olds are so, so old,
and I think what better fate could you
have than whatever she foresees?)

There will be jars for her as well
        some day
but I will not see them or store them
        like my father-in-law's ashes
confined and nomadic in our moves
        from Wisconsin to the Deep South.
The man should be buried in Chicago,
        or cast to the winds down Belle Plaine
Avenue, but he is here, still, twelve years after
        his surprising death, a heart attack
while bagging leaves in his front lawn
        one autumn day, and so he is vased
in my wife's art studio.

V.

The liver, oh, the timbre of my organs,
        the Hammond B-3 in Booker T's MGs,
a soul song from Stash that is the organ
        of the soundtrack of my liver—taut,
no, most likely not,
        but deep brown or red, and slick,
pocked by, I imagine, a parking lot
        of empty bottles: the Bacardi of my first drunks,

not technically my very first, that mix of white wine
          and apple cider stolen by a childhood friend
from his parents' party, tossed off their porch
          into an alley where I caught the plastic milk cartons
filled with the sweet concoction and drank it
          on the island median of our parents' avenue
and let the concrete and grass spin and spin.
          This was Madison, in 1979,
and everyone I loved was still alive
          or yet to be born.

Cardboard cases of returnable Miller bottles,
          Point, Leinie's, Mickey's Big Mouth, and later
tequila, tequila, tequila, then gin and whiskey,
          my autobiography in alcohol,
but I am lucky: it never kills me,
          though it tries three times, but booze strikes out.

Thy bread is to thee.
          Thy beer is to thee.
Thou livest upon that on which Ra lives

VI.

Four jars, I dream, pots of plain design,
          Sam Cooke's lungs, the intestines of Orson Welles,
Elvis Presley's stomach, Dorothy Parker's kidneys,
          lined up on the mantel of Thornton Wilder's childhood
home, a house I painted when I dropped out of college, scraping,
          then blowing leaded paint dust out of my nose, so much
dust, so much (and the men preparing the Pharaoh's corpse pulled
          the brains

out of the skull with long needles and yanked it through
            the nostrils) and now I'm in the Magic Treehouse
with Jack and Annie listening to Billie Holiday sing
            from *Book-of-the-Month* club vinyl, wondering
what do kidneys do? And staring at a faded photo
            of a long dead aunt, the one who my father wouldn't talk
about and she's smiling in a wool plaid shirt with a passel
            of Labrador puppies crowded in her arms and she died
with a dime in her pocket on the streets of St. Paul
            (and that's all your mother knew)

and this is what sorrow looks like, the smiling girl
and the long-dead dogs,
and my father's silence over supper
and her organs lost to some Minnesota cemetery
lungs, kidneys, intestines, and stomach
baboon and jackal and falcon and man,
baboon and jackal and falcon and woman,
those are the gods who will tend us
those are the gods who will mend us

We have two cats, not gods
            but worthy of preservation:
opened up, polished out, divvied up, tended
once baboon and jackal and falcon,
now cat, and of course, cat.

117

VII.

There is a jar buried in a hillside in Tennessee
        and there are ships in bottles and pennies
in piggy-banks waiting the smash of the hammer
        and charity-raising car demolition
ten dollars for ten swings.

        Shatter the windshield, take out the tail light
bat the side mirror into the dead grass
        beside the churning carousel
behind the midway vendors
the sides of the Chevy spray-painted
        with a slogan: *Stick it to Cancer!*
as if cancer were this sad car,
        or maybe cancer is a car:
a journey,
        driven and driven and dead.

So: disembowel me, I guess:
        stash a piece of me in the glove compartment
of a red 1981 Nova
        and another in the open back of a Marshall amp,
sliced and slivered and dried, then slipped
        between the pages of my books, dozens
on dozens on dozens. I'll let you choose
        the titles. Surprise me.
Or wait: consider the elementary school
        art project—sand in a jar, multi-hued,
grades of blue and red and green
        and yellow, layer on layer.
Burn me, after all. Color me.
        Powdered dye of my eyes, my ears,
my throat, I can think of so many parts

cherished beyond the torso organs.
My lips, my tongue:
        talk and lick and kiss.

VIII.

She wakes at one-fifteen
        and calls for me:
"Daddy, I had a night mirror.
        A shark bit me. Stay with me."
We lay on her narrow bed
        the sole red shadows
from the ladybug night-light,
        plastic and stamped *Made in China.*
The shadows of her dresser-top,
        souvenir tea pot and tchotchke box,
sequined chest of bobby pins and hair ties.

Maybe I will end there.
        But all the boxes are too small.
I look at her and the earth shakes.
        Whatever I feel has no small walls
but my skin, and what our skin
        contains is so much less than what we live.
The planet has spun
        for half a century with me on it
and I won't see her reach my age.
        I age in stages more apparent,
true apparition in the night mirror.
        Shower and shave and survive
no, more than survive,
        for this more than love.

Hathor, goddess of love,
        I don't need another life
unless I have this child in it,
        the tomb of my heart
incomplete without her.

        I am jigsawed already
eating stray gray hairs,
        living with my trembling blood
and my already jarred heart.

About the Author

John A. McDermott is a native of Madison, Wisconsin. He is also the author of *The Idea of God in Tennessee* (Kelsay Books 2015). He is married to the writer and editor, Christine Butterworth-McDermott.

www.ingramcontent.com/pod-product-compliance
Lightning Source LLC
Chambersburg PA
CBHW032105080426
42733CB00006B/421